Note to Educators and Parents

Reading is such an exciting adventure for young children! They are beginning to integrate their oral language skills with written language. To help this process along, books must be meaningful, colorful, engaging, and interesting; they should invite young readers to make inquiries about the world around them.

Months of the Year is a new series of books designed to help children learn more about each of the twelve months. In each book, young readers will learn about festivals, celebrations, weather, and other interesting facts about each month.

Each book is specially designed to support the young reader in the reading process. The familiar topics are appealing to young children and invite them to re-read — again and again. The full-color photographs and enhanced text further support the student during the reading process.

These books are designed to be read within an instructional guided reading group. This small group setting allows beginning readers to work with a fluent adult model as they make meaning from the text. After children develop fluency with the text and content, the book can be read independently. Children and adults alike will find these books supportive, engaging, and fun!

— *Susan Nations, M.Ed., author, literacy coach,*
and consultant in literacy development

November is the eleventh month of the year. November has 30 days.

November 11

1	2	3	4	5	6	7
8	9	10	11	12	13	14
15	16	17	18	19	20	21
22	23	24	25	26	27	28
29	30					

November is a fall month. In some places, the weather begins to get cold.

Is it cold in November where you live?

Election Day usually occurs early in November. This is when adults have a chance to choose some of the people who run the government.

November 11 is Veterans Day. It is a holiday to celebrate the end of two world wars and to honor the people who fought in all wars.

The fourth Thursday in November is Thanksgiving. On Thanksgiving, people give thanks for the good things they have in their lives.

Thanksgiving is also a time to be thankful for all the vegetables and fruits that have been grown and eaten. November is when the last of the crops are picked.

People like to prepare and eat special foods for Thanksgiving. Some special foods are turkey, yams, potatoes, corn, squash, cranberries, and pumpkin pie for dessert.

On Thanksgiving, many people celebrate by having a big dinner with family and friends.

What is your favorite food on Thanksgiving?

When November ends,
it is time for December to
begin. Soon it will be
time for winter.

Glossary

crops — vegetables, fruits, and other plants that are grown to be used for food

pie — a traditional American dessert that has crust as the bottom and fruit or vegetables as the filling

Thanksgiving — a holiday when families and friends give thanks and get together for a special meal

Months of the Year

1	January	7	July
2	February	8	August
3	March	9	September
4	April	10	October
5	May	**11**	**November**
6	June	12	December

Seasons of the Year

Winter	Summer
Spring	Fall

About the Author

Robyn Brode wrote the *Going Places* children's book series and was the editor for *Get Out!*, which won the 2002 Disney Award for Hands-On Activities. She has been an editor, writer, and teacher in the book publishing field for many years. She earned a Bachelors in English Literature from the University of California at Berkeley.